A Gardener's Miscellany

A GARDENER'S MISCELLANY

Summersdale Publishers Ltd
46 West Street
Chichester
West Sussex
PO19 1RP
UK

www.summersdale.com

Printed and bound in China

ISBN: 978-1-84953-260-0

Substantial discounts on bulk quantities of Summersdale books are available to corporations, professional associations and other organisations. For details telephone Summersdale Publishers on (+44-1243-771107), fax (+44-1243-786300) or email (nicky@summersdale.com).

A Gardener's Miscellany

CONTENTS

I value my garden more for
being full of blackbirds than
of cherries, and very frankly
give them fruit for their songs.

JOSEPH ADDISON

As spring came on, a new set of amusements became the fashion, and the lengthening days gave long afternoons for work and play of all sorts. The garden had to be put in order, and each sister had a quarter of the little plot to do what she liked with. Hannah used to say, 'I'd know which each of them gardings belonged to, 'ef I see 'em in Chiny,' and so she might, for the girls' tastes differed as much as their characters. Meg's had roses and heliotrope, myrtle, and a little orange tree in it. Jo's bed was never alike two seasons, for she was always trying experiments. This year it was to be a plantation of sun flowers, the seeds of which cheerful land-aspiring plant were to feed Aunt Cockle-top and her family of chicks. Beth had old-fashioned fragrant flowers in her garden, sweet peas and mignonette, larkspur, pinks, pansies, and southernwood, with chickweed for the birds and catnip for the pussies. Amy had a bower in hers, rather small and earwiggy, but very pretty to look at, with honeysuckle and morning-glories hanging their coloured horns and bells in graceful wreaths all over it, tall white lilies, delicate ferns, and as many brilliant, picturesque plants as would consent to blossom there.

LOUISA MAY ALCOTT, *LITTLE WOMEN*

The longer I live the greater is my
respect and affection for manure.

ELIZABETH VON ARNIM

May 7th.

I love my garden. I am writing in it now in the late afternoon loveliness, much interrupted by the mosquitoes and the temptation to look at all the glories of the new green leaves washed half an hour ago in a cold shower. Two owls are perched near me, and are carrying on a long conversation that I enjoy as much as any warbling of nightingales.

ELIZABETH VON ARNIM,
ELIZABETH AND HER GERMAN GARDEN

When the world wearies, and society ceases
to satisfy, there is always the garden.

MINNIE AUMÔNIER

To sit in the shade on a fine day and look upon verdure is the most perfect refreshment.

JANE AUSTEN, *MANSFIELD PARK*

Mr Collins invited them to take a stroll in the garden, which was large and well laid out, and to the cultivation of which he attended himself. To work in his garden was one of his most respectable pleasures... Here, leading the way through every walk and cross walk, and scarcely allowing them an interval to utter the praises he asked for, every view was pointed out with a minuteness which left beauty entirely behind.

JANE AUSTEN, *PRIDE AND PREJUDICE*

There is no gardening without humility. Nature is constantly sending even its oldest scholars to the bottom of the class for some egregious blunder.

ALFRED AUSTIN

So, summoning a south-west wind, still bearing in his garments the odours of the tropic bowers where he had slept, the fair day descended softly in his arms to earth, and, seating herself upon the hills, wove a drapery of golden mist, bright as love, and tender as maidenhood. Then, wrapped in this bridal veil, she floated, still in the arms of the gentle wind, through the forests, touching their leaves with purer gold and richer crimson; over the harvest-fields, whose shocks of lingering corn rustled responsive as her trailing garments swept past; over wide, brown pastures, where the cattle nibbled luxuriously at the sweet after-math; over lakes and rivers, where the waters slept content, forgetting, for the moment, their restless seaward march; over sheltered gardens, where hollyhock and sunflower, petunia and pansy, dahlia and phlox, whispering together of the summer vanished and the frosty nights at hand, gave out the mysterious, melancholy perfume of an autumn day.

JANE GOODWIN AUSTIN, *OUTPOST*

Gardening is the purest
of human pleasures.

SIR FRANCIS BACON

23

The garden is best to be square, encompassed on all the four sides with a stately arched hedge. The arches to be upon pillars of carpenter's work, of some ten foot high and six foot broad; and the spaces between of the same dimension with the breadth of the arch. Over the arches let there be an entire hedge, of some four foot high, framed also upon carpenter's work; and upon the upper hedge, over every arch, a little turret, with a belly, enough to receive a cage of birds; and over every space between the arches some other little figure, with broad plates of round coloured glass, gilt, for the sun to play upon. But this hedge I intend to be raised upon a bank, not steep, but gently slope, of some six foot, set all with flowers. Also I understand, that this square of the garden should not be the whole breadth of the ground, but to leave, on either side, ground enough for diversity of side alleys; unto which the two covert alleys of the green may deliver you. But there must be no alleys with hedges at either end of this great enclosure: not at the hither end, for letting your prospect upon this fair hedge from the green; nor at the further end, for letting your prospect from the hedge, through the arches upon the heath.

SIR FRANCIS BACON, 'OF GARDENS'

What a desolate place would
be a world without a flower! It
would be a face without a smile,
a feast without a welcome.

A. J. BALFOUR

from The Deserted Garden

I mind me in the days departed,
How often underneath the sun
With childish bounds I used to run
To a garden long deserted.

The beds and walks were vanished quite;
And wheresoe'er had struck the spade,
The greenest grasses Nature laid,
To sanctify her right.

I called the place my wilderness,
For no one entered there but I,
The sheep looked in, the grass to espy,
And passed it ne'ertheless.

The trees were interwoven wild,
And spread their boughs enough about
To keep both sheep and shepherd out,
But not a happy child.

Adventurous joy it was for me!
I crept beneath the boughs, and found
A circle smooth of mossy ground
Beneath a poplar tree.

Old garden rose-trees hedged it in,
Bedropt with roses waxen-white
Well satisfied with dew and light
And careless to be seen.

ELIZABETH BARRETT BROWNING

Flowers have an expression of countenance as much as men or animals. Some seem to smile; some have a sad expression; some are pensive and diffident; others again are plain, honest and upright, like the broad-faced sunflower and the hollyhock.

HENRY WARD BEECHER

from Ah! Sun-flower!

Ah, Sun-flower! weary of time,
Who countest the steps of the Sun:
Seeking after that sweet golden clime,
Where the traveller's journey is done.

WILLIAM BLAKE

How beautiful the whole garden looked at the hour when it should have been night, about ten o'clock, in the strange, weirdly daylight! Beyond the high west line of wall and the trees at the upper end, in the cold clear sky lay level flakes of cloud, fired by a sunset glow.

ELEANOR VERE BOYLE, *SYLVANA'S LETTERS TO AN UNKNOWN FRIEND*

from The Garden in September

Now thin mists temper the slow-ripening beams
Of the September sun: his golden gleams
On gaudy flowers shine, that prank the rows
Of high-grown hollyhocks, and all tall shows
That Autumn flaunteth in his bushy bowers;
Where tomtits, hanging from the drooping heads
Of giant sunflowers, peck the nutty seeds;
And in the feathery aster bees on wing
Seize and set free the honied flowers,

Till thousand stars leap with their visiting:

While ever across the path mazily flit,

Unpiloted in the sun,

The dreamy butterflies

With dazzling colours powdered and soft glooms,

White, black and crimson stripes, and peacock eyes,

Or on chance flowers sit,

With idle effort plundering one by one

The nectaries of deepest-throated blooms.

ROBERT BRIDGES

from The Testament of Beauty

I know that if odour were visible, as colour is,
I'd see the summer garden in rainbow clouds.

ROBERT BRIDGES

How beautiful a garden is when all the fruit-trees are in bloom, and how various that bloom is! Each Pear-tree bears a different blossom from its neighbour, and the handsomest of all, in size and shape of flower and form of cluster, is the Jargonelle. But no Pear-blossom can compare with the beauty of blossom on the Apple-trees; and of all Apple-trees the Pomeroy is most beautiful, when every bough is laden with clusters of deep-red buds, which shade off into the softest rosy white as, one by one, the blossoms open out.

HENRY BRIGHT, *A YEAR IN A LANCASHIRE GARDEN*

The garden was a large one, and tastefully laid out; besides several splendid dahlias, there were some other fine flowers still in bloom: but my companion would not give me time to examine them: I must go with him, across the wet grass, to a remote sequestered corner, the most important place in the grounds, because it contained *his* garden. There were two round beds, stocked with a variety of plants. In one there was a pretty little rose-tree. I paused to admire its lovely blossoms.

ANNE BRONTË, *AGNES GREY*

While such honey-dew fell, such silence reigned, such gloaming gathered, I felt as if I could haunt such shade for ever: but in threading the flower and fruit-parterres at the upper part of the enclosure, enticed there by the light the now-rising moon cast on this more open quarter, my step is stayed – not by sound, not by sight, but once more by a warning fragrance.

Sweet briar and southernwood, jasmine, pink, and rose, have long been yielding their evening sacrifice of incense: this new scent is neither of shrub nor flower; it is – I know it well – it is Mr Rochester's cigar.

CHARLOTTE BRONTË, *JANE EYRE*

Spring evenings are often cold and raw, and though this had been a fine day, warm even in the morning and meridian sunshine, the air chilled at sunset, the ground crisped, and ere dusk a hoar frost was insidiously stealing over growing grass and unfolding bud. It whitened the pavement in front of Briarmains (Mr Yorke's residence), and made silent havoc among the tender plants in his garden, and on the mossy level of his lawn. As to that great tree, strong-trunked and broad-armed, which guarded the gable nearest the road, it seemed to defy a spring-night frost to harm its still-bare boughs; and so did the leafless grove of walnut-trees rising tall behind the house.

CHARLOTTE BRONTË, *SHIRLEY*

from A Little Budding Rose

It was a little budding rose,
Round like a fairy globe,
And shyly did its leaves unclose
Hid in their mossy robe,
But sweet was the slight and spicy smell
It breathed from its heart invisible.

EMILY BRONTË

The Bluebell

The Bluebell is the sweetest flower
That waves in summer air:
Its blossoms have the mightiest power
To soothe my spirit's care.

There is a spell in purple heath
Too wildly, sadly dear;
The violet has a fragrant breath
But fragrance will not cheer,

The trees are bare, the sun is cold,
And seldom, seldom seen;
The heavens have lost their zone of gold,
And earth her robe of green.

And ice upon the glancing stream
Has cast its sombre shade;
And distant hills and valleys seem
In frozen mist arrayed.

The Bluebell cannot charm me now,
　　The heath has lost its bloom;
　　The violets in the glen below,
　　They yield no sweet perfume.

But, though I mourn the sweet Bluebell,
　　'Tis better far away;
I know how fast my tears would swell
　　To see it smile to-day.

For, oh! when chill the sunbeams fall
　　Adown that dreary sky,
And gild yon dank and darkened wall
　　With transient brilliancy;

How do I weep, how do I pine
　　For the time of flowers to come,
And turn me from that fading shine,
　　To mourn the fields of home!

EMILY BRONTË

On a mellow evening in September, I was coming from the garden with a heavy basket of apples which I had been gathering. It had got dusk, and the moon looked over the high wall of the court, causing undefined shadows to lurk in the corners of the numerous projecting portions of the building. I set my burden on the house-steps by the kitchen-door, and lingered to rest, and drew in a few more breaths of the soft, sweet air; my eyes were on the moon, and my back to the entrance, when I heard a voice behind me say, – 'Nelly, is that you?'

EMILY BRONTË, *WUTHERING HEIGHTS*

The Rose

A rose, as fair as ever saw the North,
Grew in a little garden all alone;
A sweeter flower did Nature ne'er put forth,
Nor fairer garden yet was never known:
The maidens danced about it morn and noon,
And learnèd bards of it their ditties made;
The nimble fairies by the pale-faced moon
Water'd the root and kiss'd her pretty shade.
But well-a-day! – the gardener careless grew;
The maids and fairies both were kept away,
And in a drought the caterpillars threw
Themselves upon the bud and every spray.
God shield the stock! If heaven send no supplies,
The fairest blossom of the garden dies.

WILLIAM BROWNE

from The Planting of the Apple-Tree

Come, let us plant the apple-tree.
Cleave the tough greensward with the spade;
Wide let its hollow bed be made;
There gently lay the roots, and there
Sift the dark mould with kindly care,
And press it o'er them tenderly,
As, round the sleeping infant's feet,
We softly fold the cradle-sheet;
So plant we the apple-tree.

What plant we in this apple-tree?
Buds, which the breath of summer days
Shall lengthen into leafy sprays;
Boughs where the thrush, with crimson breast,
Shall haunt and sing and hide her nest;
We plant, upon the sunny lea,
A shadow for the noontide hour,
A shelter from the summer shower,
When we plant the apple-tree.

What plant we in this apple-tree?
Sweets for a hundred flowery springs
To load the May-wind's restless wings,
When, from the orchard row, he pours
Its fragrance through our open doors;
A world of blossoms for the bee,
Flowers for the sick girl's silent room,
For the glad infant sprigs of bloom,
We plant with the apple-tree.

What plant we in this apple-tree?
Fruits that shall swell in sunny June,
And redden in the August noon,
And drop, when gentle airs come by,
That fan the blue September sky,
While children come, with cries of glee,
And seek them where the fragrant grass
Betrays their bed to those who pass,
At the foot of the apple-tree.

WILLIAM CULLEN BRYANT

from Upon a Snail

She goes but softly, but she goeth sure;
She stumbles not, as stronger creatures do;
Her journey's shorter, so she may endure
Better than they which do much farther go.

She makes no noise, but stilly seizeth on
The flower or herb appointed for her food,
The which she quietly doth feed upon,
While others range and glare, but find no good.

And though she doth but very softly go,
However 'tis not fast, nor slow, but sure;
And certainly they that do travel so,
The prize they do aim at they do procure.

JOHN BUNYAN

'I wouldn't want to make it look like a gardener's garden, all clipped an' spick an' span, would you?' he said. 'It's nicer like this with things runnin' wild, an' swingin' an' catchin' hold of each other.'

FRANCES HODGSON BURNETT, *THE SECRET GARDEN*

When Rosy May

When rosy May comes in wi' flowers,
To deck her gay, green-spreading bowers,
Then busy, busy are his hours,
The gard'ner wi' his paidle.

The crystal waters gently fa',
The merry birds are lovers a',
The scented breezes round him blaw –
The gard'ner wi' his paidle.

When purple morning starts the hare
To steal upon her early fare;
Then thro' the dews he maun repair –
The gard'ner wi' his paidle.

When Day, expiring in the west,
The curtain draws o' Nature's rest,
He flies to her arms he lo'es the best,
The gard'ner wi' his paidle.

ROBERT BURNS

'O Tiger-lily,' said Alice, addressing herself to one that was waving gracefully about in the wind, 'I *wish* you could talk!'

'We *can* talk,' said the Tiger-lily, 'when there's anybody worth talking to.'

Alice was so astonished that she couldn't speak for a minute: it quite seemed to take her breath away. At length, as the Tiger-lily only went on waving about, she spoke again, in a timid voice – almost in a whisper. 'And can *all* the flowers talk?'

'As well as *you* can,' said the Tiger-lily. 'And a great deal louder.'

'It isn't manners for us to begin, you know,' said the Rose, 'and I really was wondering when you'd speak! Said I to myself, "Her face has got *some* sense in it, though it's not a clever one!" Still you're the right colour, and that goes a long way.'

'I don't care about the colour,' the Tiger-lily remarked. 'If only her petals curled up a little more, she'd be all right.'

LEWIS CARROLL, *THROUGH THE LOOKING-GLASS, AND WHAT ALICE FOUND THERE*

Robin

The sparrow seeks his feathers for a nest
And the fond robin with his ruddy breast
Hops round the garden wall were thickly twine
The leafing sweet briar and the propt woodbine
And in a hole behind the thickening boughs
He builds with hopeful joy his little house
Stealing with jealous speed the wool and hair
Were cows and sheep have lain them down to lair
And pecks the green moss in his murmuring glee
From cottage thatch and squatting apple tree
Tutling his song –

JOHN CLARE

If well managed, nothing is more beautiful than the kitchen-garden: the earliest blossoms come there: we shall in vain seek for flowering shrubs in March, and early in April, to equal the peaches, nectarines, apricots and plums; late in April, we shall find nothing to equal the pear and the cherry; and, in May, the dwarf, or espalier, apple-trees, are just so many immense garlands of carnations.

WILLIAM COBBETT, *THE ENGLISH GARDENER*

The Months

January brings the snow,
Makes our feet and fingers glow.

February brings the rain,
Thaws the frozen lake again.

March brings breezes loud and shrill,
Stirs the dancing daffodil.

April brings the primrose sweet,
Scatters daisies at our feet.

May brings flocks of pretty lambs,
Skipping by their fleecy dams.

June brings tulips, lilies, roses,
Fills the children's hands with posies.

Hot July brings cooling showers,
Apricots and gillyflowers.

August brings the sheaves of corn,
Then the harvest home is borne.

Warm September brings the fruit,
Sportsmen then begin to shoot.

Fresh October brings the pheasant,
Then to gather nuts is pleasant.

Dull November brings the blast,
Then the leaves are whirling fast.

Chill December brings the sleet,
Blazing fire, and Christmas treat.

SARA COLERIDGE

My greenhouse is never so pleasant as when we are just on the point of being turned out of it. The gentleness of the autumnal suns, and the calmness of this latter season, make it a much more agreeable retreat than we ever find it in summer... I sit with all the windows and the door wide open, and am regaled with the scent of every flower in a garden as full of flowers as I have known how to make it.

WILLIAM COWPER, LETTER TO THE REV. JOHN NEWTON, 18 SEPTEMBER 1784

... In fine weather the old gentleman is almost constantly in the garden, and when it is too wet to go into it, he will look out of the window at it, by the hour together. He has always something to do there, and you will see him digging, and sweeping, and cutting, and planting, with manifest delight. In spring-time there is no end to the sowing of seeds, and sticking little bits of wood over them, with labels, which look like epitaphs to their memory; and in the evening, when the sun has gone down, the perseverance with which he lugs a great watering-pot about is perfectly astonishing.

CHARLES DICKENS, *SKETCHES BY BOZ*

The pedigree of honey......Does not concern the bee:......A clover, any time, to him......Is aristocracy......Emily Dickinson......

The moonbeam fell upon the roof and garden of Gerard. It suffused the cottage with its brilliant light, except where the dark depth of the embowered porch defied its entry. All around the beds of flowers and herbs spread sparkling and defined. You could trace the minutest walk; almost distinguish every leaf. Now and then there came a breath, and the sweet-peas murmured in their sleep; or the roses rustled, as if they were afraid they were about to be roused from their lightsome dreams. Farther on the fruit-trees caught the splendour of the night; and looked like a troop of sultanas taking their gardened air, when the eye of man could not profane them, and laden with jewels. There were apples that rivalled rubies; pears of topaz tint; a whole paraphernalia of plums, some purple as the amethyst, others blue and brilliant as the sapphire; an emerald here, and now a golden drop that gleamed like the yellow diamond of Genghis Khan.

BENJAMIN DISRAELI, *SYBIL*

the confused leafage of a hedgerow bank, as a more gladdening sight than the finest cistus or fuchsia spreading itself on the softest undulating turf, is an entirely unjustifiable preference to a nursery-gardener, or to any of those regulated minds who are free from the weakness of any attachment that does not rest on a demonstrable superiority of qualities. And there is no better reason for preferring this elderberry bush than that it stirs an early memory; that it is no novelty in my life, speaking to me merely through my present sensibilities to form and colour, but the long companion of my existence, that wove itself into my joys when joys were vivid.

GEORGE ELIOT, *THE MILL ON THE FLOSS*

The garden is never dead; growth is always going on, and growth that can be seen, and seen with delight.

HENRY ELLACOMBE, *IN MY VICARAGE GARDEN*

Who has learned to garden
who did not at the same
time learn to be patient?

H. L. V. FLETCHER

from The Feat of Gardening

How so well a gardener be,
Here he may both hear and see
Every time of the year and of the moon
And how the crafte shall be done,
In what manner he shall delve and set
Both in drought and in wet,
How he shall his seeds sow;
Of every month he must know
Both of wortes and of leek,
Onions and of garlic,
Parsley, clary and eke sage
And all other herbage.

JOHN GARDENER

The garden lay close under the house; a bright spot enough by day; for in that soil, whatever was planted grew and blossomed in spite of neglect. The white roses glimmered out in the dusk all the night through; the red were lost in shadow. Between the low boundary of the garden and the hills swept one or two green meadows; Ruth looked into the grey darkness till she traced each separate wave of outline. Then she heard a little restless bird chirp out its wakefulness from a nest in the ivy round the walls of the house. But the mother-bird spread her soft feathers, and hushed it into silence. Presently, however, many little birds began to scent the coming dawn, and rustled among the leaves, and chirruped loud and clear. Just above the horizon, too, the mist became a silvery grey cloud hanging on the edge of the world; presently it turned shimmering white; and then, in an instant, it flushed into rose, and the mountain-tops sprang into heaven, and bathed in the presence of the shadow of God. With a bound, the sun of a molten fiery red came above the horizon, and immediately thousands of little birds sang out for joy, and a soft chorus of mysterious, glad murmurs came forth from the earth; the low whispering wind left its hiding-place among the clefts and hollows of the hills, and wandered among the rustling herbs and trees, waking the flower-buds to the life of another day.

ELIZABETH GASKELL, *RUTH*

Nature is all very well in her place, but she must not be allowed to make things untidy.

STELLA GIBBONS, *COLD COMFORT FARM*

My Neighbour's Roses

The roses red upon my neighbour's vine
Are owned by him, but they are also mine.
His was the cost, and his the labour, too,
But mine as well as his the joy,
their loveliness to view.

They bloom for me and are for me as fair
As for the man who gives them all his care.
Thus I am rich, because a good man grew
A rose-clad vine for all his neighbours' view.

I know from this that others plant for me,

And what they own, my joy may also be.

So why be selfish, when so much that's fine

Is grown for you, upon your neighbour's vine.

ABRAHAM L. GRUBER

from God's Garden

The kiss of the sun for pardon,
The song of the birds for mirth,
One is nearer God's
heart in a garden
Than anywhere else on earth.

DOROTHY FRANCES GURNEY

Arise, arise, arise!

And pick your love a posy,

All o' the sweetest flowers

That in the garden grow.

The turtle doves and sma' birds

In every bough a-building,

So early in the May-time,

At the break o' the day!

THOMAS HARDY, *TESS OF THE D'URBERVILLES*

I used to visit and revisit it a dozen times a day, and stand in deep contemplation over my vegetable progeny with a love that nobody could share or conceive of who had never taken part in the process of creation. It was one of the most bewitching sights in the world to observe a hill of beans thrusting aside the soil, or a rose of early peas just peeping forth sufficiently to trace a line of delicate green.

NATHANIEL HAWTHORNE, *MOSSES FROM AN OLD MANSE*

To a Bed of Tulips

Bright tulips, we do know
You had your coming hither,
And fading-time does show
That ye must quickly wither.

Your sisterhoods may stay,
And smile here for your hour;
But die ye must away,
Even as the meanest flower.

Come, virgins, then, and see
Your frailties; and bemoan ye;
For, lost like these, 'twill be
As time had never known ye.

ROBERT HERRICK

To Blossoms

Fair pledges of a fruitful tree,
Why do ye fall so fast?
Your date is not so past,
But you may stay yet here awhile,
To blush and gently smile,
And go at last.

What! were ye born to be
An hour or half's delight,
And so to bid good night?
'Tis pity nature brought ye forth,
Merely to show your worth,
And lose you quite.

But you are lovely leaves, where we
May read how soon things have
Their end, though ne'er so brave:
And after they have shown their pride,
Like you, awhile, they glide
Into the grave.

ROBERT HERRICK

The plot of earth which he called his garden was celebrated in the town for the beauty of the flowers which he cultivated there... By dint of labour, of perseverance, of attention, and of buckets of water, he had succeeded in creating after the Creator, and he had invented certain tulips and certain dahlias which seemed to have been forgotten by nature.

VICTOR HUGO, *LES MISÉRABLES*

There were the smoothest lawns in the world stretching down to the edge of this liquid slowness and making, where the water touched them, a line as even as the rim of a champagne-glass... The place was a garden of delight.

HENRY JAMES, *ENGLISH HOURS*

He rambled an hour, in a state of breathless ecstasy; brushing the dew from the deep fern and bracken and the rich borders of the garden, tasting the fragrant air and stopping everywhere in murmuring rapture, at the touch of some exquisite impression. His whole walk was peopled with recognitions; he had been dreaming all his life of just such a place and such objects, such a morning and such a chance. It was the last of April, and everything was fresh and vivid; the great trees, in the early air, were a blur of tender shoots. Round the admirable house he revolved repeatedly, catching every point and tone, feasting on its expression... There was something in the way the grey walls rose from the green lawn that brought tears to his eyes.

HENRY JAMES, *THE PRINCESS CASAMASSIMA*

from On a Fine Crop of Peas being Spoil'd by a Storm

When Morrice views his prostrate peas,
By raging whirlwinds spread,
He wrings his hands, and in amaze
He sadly shakes his head.

Is this the fruit of my fond toil,
My joy, my pride, my cheer!
Shall one tempestuous hour thus spoil
The labours of a year!

Oh! what avails, that day by day
I nursed the thriving crop,
And settled with my foot the clay,
And reared the social prop!

Ambition's pride had spurred me on
All gard'ners to excel.
I often called them one by one,
And boastingly would tell,

How I prepared the furrowed ground
And how the grain did sow,
Then challenged all the country round
For such an early blow.

How did their bloom my wishes raise!
What hopes did they afford,
To earn my honoured master's praise,
And crown his cheerful board!

Poor Morrice, wrapt in sad surprise,
Demands in sober mood,
'Should storms molest a man so wise,
A man so just and good?

Ah! Morrice, cease thy fruitless moan,
Nor at misfortunes spurn,
Misfortune's not thy lot alone;
Each neighbour hath his turn.

HENRY JONES

On the Grasshopper and Cricket

The poetry of earth is never dead:
When all the birds are faint with the hot sun,
And hide in cooling trees, a voice will run
From hedge to hedge about the new-mown mead;
That is the Grasshopper's – he takes the lead
In summer luxury, – he has never done
With his delights; for when tired out with fun,
He rests at ease beneath some pleasant weed.
The poetry of earth is ceasing never:
On a lone winter evening, when the frost
Has wrought a silence, from the stove there shrills
The Cricket's song, in warmth increasing ever,
And seems to one in drowsiness half lost,
The Grasshopper's among some grassy hills.

John Keats

Trees

I think that I shall never see
A poem lovely as a tree.

A tree whose hungry mouth is presst
Against the earth's sweet flowing breast;

A tree that looks at God all day,
And lifts her leafy arms to pray;

A tree that may in summer wear
A nest of robins in her hair;

Upon whose bosom snow has lain;
Who intimately lives with rain.

Poems are made by fools like me,
But only God can make a tree.

JOYCE KILMER

A Contemplation Upon Flowers

Brave flowers – that I could gallant it like you,
And be as little vain!
You come abroad, and make a harmless show,
And to your beds of earth again.
You are not proud: you know your birth:
For your embroider'd garments are from earth.

You do obey your months and times, but I
Would have it ever Spring:
My fate would know no Winter, never die,
Nor think of such a thing.
O that I could my bed of earth but view
And smile, and look as cheerfully as you!

O teach me to see Death and not to fear,
But rather to take truce!
How often have I seen you at bier,
And there look fresh and spruce!
You fragrant flowers! then teach me, that my breath
Like yours may sweeten and perfume my death.

HENRY KING, BISHOP OF CHICHESTER

from The Glory of the Garden

Our England is a garden that is full of stately views,
Of borders, beds and shrubberies
and lawns and avenues,
With statues on the terraces and peacocks strutting by;
But the Glory of the Garden lies in
more than meets the eye.

For where the old thick laurels grow,
along the thin red wall,
You will find the tool- and potting-
sheds which are the heart of all;
The cold-frames and the hot-houses,
the dungpits and the tanks:
The rollers, carts and drain-pipes, with
the barrows and the planks.

And there you'll see the gardeners,
the men and 'prentice boys
Told off to do as they are bid and do it without noise;
For, except when seeds are planted
and we shout to scare the birds,
The Glory of the Garden it abideth not in words.

And some can pot begonias and some can bud a rose,
And some are hardly fit to trust
with anything that grows;
But they can roll and trim the lawns
and sift the sand and loam,
For the Glory of the Garden occupieth all who come.

RUDYARD KIPLING

A half-moon, dusky gold, was sinking behind the black sycamore at the end of the garden, making the sky dull purple with its glow. Nearer, a dim white fence of lilies went across the garden, and the air all round seemed to stir with scent... He went across the beds of pinks, whose keen perfume came sharply across the rocking, heavy scent of the lilies, and stood alongside the white barrier of flowers. They flagged all loose, as if they were panting. The scent made him drunk.

D. H. Lawrence, *Sons and Lovers*

It is a greater act of faith to plant a bulb than to plant a tree... to see in these wizened, colourless shapes the subtle curves of the iris reticulata or the tight locks of the hyacinth.

CLARE LEIGHTON,
FOUR HEDGES: A GARDENER'S CHRONICLE

Against the house may be planted currants, pears, or a vine, according to the situation and climate. Honeysuckles and monthly roses may be planted next to the porch; ivy against the water-closet; and the scented climatis against the pigstye. The border round the house should be devoted to savoury pot-herbs, as parsley, thyme, mint chives, &c. and to flowers and low flowering shrubs. The surrounding border, under the wall or hedge, should be devoted to early and late culinary crops, as early potatoes, pease, turnips, kidney-beans, &c. No forest trees, especially the ash and elm, should be planted in, or if possible, even near the cottager's garden; as these are ruinous to crops; the first both by its shade and roots, and the latter by its roots, which spread rapidly to a great extent, close under the surface. The oak is the tree the least injurious to gardens.

JOHN CLAUDIUS LOUDON,
AN ENCYCLOPAEDIA OF GARDENING

To watch the season through, to lose myself in love of the earth – that is Life to me. I don't feel I could ever live in a city again. First the bare tree, then the buds and the flowers, then the leaves, then the small fruit forming and swelling. If I only watch one tree a year one is richer for life.

KATHERINE MANSFIELD, LETTER TO RICHARD MURRY, 20 JUNE 1921

from The Garden

What wondrous life is this I lead!
Ripe apples drop about my head;
The luscious clusters of the vine
Upon my mouth do crush their wine;
The nectarine and curious peach
Into my hands themselves do reach;
Stumbling on melons as I pass,
Insnared with flowers, I fall on grass.

Meanwhile the mind, from pleasure less,
Withdraws into its happiness:
The mind, that ocean where each kind
Does straight its own resemblance find;
Yet it creates, transcending these,
Far other worlds, and other seas;
Annihilating all that's made
To a green thought in a green shade.

Here at the fountain's sliding foot,
Or at some fruit-tree's mossy root,
Casting the body's vest aside,
My soul into the boughs does glide:
There like a bird it sits and sings,
Then whets and combs its silver wings;
And, till prepared for longer flight,
Waves in its plumes the various light.

Such was that happy garden-state,
While man there walked without a mate:
After a place so pure and sweet,
What other help could yet be meet!
But 'twas beyond a mortal's share
To wander solitary there:
Two paradises 'twere in one
To live in Paradise alone.

How well the skillful gard'ner drew
Of flowers and herbs this dial new;
Where from above the milder sun
Does through a fragrant zodiac run;
And, as it works, th' industrious bee
Computes its time as well as we.
How could such sweet and wholesome hours
Be reckoned but with herbs and flowers!

ANDREW MARVELL

from The Nymph Complaining For The Death of Her Faun

I have a garden of my own,

But so with roses overgrown,

And lilies, that you would it guess

To be a little wilderness.

ANDREW MARVELL

from Paradise Lost

'To the garden of bliss, thy seat prepared.'
So saying, by the hand he took me raised,
And over fields and waters, as in air
Smooth-sliding without step, last led me up
A woody mountain; whose high top was plain,
A circuit wide, enclosed, with goodliest trees
Planted, with walks, and bowers; that what I saw
Of Earth before scarce pleasant seemed. Each tree
Loaden with fairest fruit, that hung to the eye
Tempting, stirred in me sudden appetite
To pluck and eat; whereat I waked, and found
Before mine eyes all real, as the dream
Had lively shadowed.

JOHN MILTON

The pride of my heart and the delight of my eyes is my garden... I know nothing so pleasant as to sit there on a summer afternoon, with the western sun flickering through the great elder-tree, and lighting up our gay parterres, where flowers and flowering shrubs are set as thick as grass in a field, a wilderness of blossom, interwoven, intertwined, wreathy, garlandy, profuse beyond all profusion, where we may guess that there is such a thing as mould, but never see it. I know nothing so pleasant as to sit in the shade of that dark bower, with the eye resting on that bright piece of colour, lighted so gloriously by the evening sun.

MARY RUSSELL MITFORD, *OUR VILLAGE*

The many great gardens of the
world, of literature and poetry, of
painting and music, of religion and
architecture, all make the point as
clear as possible: the soul cannot
thrive in the absence of a garden.

THOMAS MORE

Large or small, it [the garden] should look both orderly and rich. It should be well fenced from the outside world. It should by no means imitate either the wilfulness or the wildness of Nature, but should look like a thing never to be seen except near a house.

WILLIAM MORRIS, *HOPES AND FEARS FOR ART*

Gardening is the art that uses flowers and plants as the paint, and the soil and sky as the canvas.

ELIZABETH MURRAY, *MONET'S PASSION*

The Daisies

In the great green park with the wooden palings –
The wooden palings so hard to climb,
There are fern and foxglove, primrose and violet,
And green things growing all the time;
And out in the open the daisies grow,
Pretty and proud in their proper places,
Millions of white-frilled daisy faces,
Millions and millions – not one or two.
And they call to the bluebells down in the wood:
'Are you out – are you in? We have been so good
All the school-time winter through,
But now it's playtime,
The gay time, the May time;
We are out and at play. Where are you?'

In the gritty garden inside the railings,
The spiky railings all painted green,
There are neat little beds of geraniums and fuchsia
With never a happy weed between.

There's a neat little grass plot, bald in places,
And very dusty to touch;
A respectable man comes once a week
To keep the garden weeded and swept,
To keep it as we don't want it kept.
He cuts the grass with his mowing-machine,
And we think he cuts it too much.
But even on the lawn, all dry and gritty,
The daisies play about.
They are so brave as well as so pretty,
You cannot keep them out.
I love them, I want to let them grow,
But that respectable man says no.
He cuts off their heads with his mowing-machine
Like the French Revolution guillotine.
He sweeps up the poor little pretty faces,
The dear little white-frilled daisy faces;
Says things must be kept in their proper places
He has no frill round his ugly face –
I wish I could find his proper place!

E. NESBIT

The Enchanted Garden

Oh, what a garden it was, living gold, living green,
Full of enchantments like spices embalming the air,
There, where you fled and I
followed – you ever unseen,
Yet each glad pulse of me cried to
my heart, 'She is there!'

Roses and lilies and lilies and roses again,
Tangle of leaves and white magic of blossoming trees,
Sunlight that lay where, last moment,
your footstep had lain –
Was not the garden enchanted
that proffered me these?

Ah, what a garden it is since I caught you at last –
Scattered the magic and shattered the spell with a kiss:
Wintry and dreary and cold with the wind of the past,
Ah that a garden enchanted should wither to this!

E. NESBIT

from An Essay on Criticism

First follow Nature, and your judgment frame
By her just standard, which is still the same:
Unerring Nature, still divinely bright,
One clear, unchang'd and universal light,
Life, force, and beauty, must to all impart,
At once the source, and end, and test of art.

ALEXANDER POPE

A gap in the hedge gave a view into the gardens; a border of jasmine, pansies and verbena, which ran along the wide path, was interplanted with fragrant wallflowers the faded rose of old Cordoba leather. A long green hose snaking across the gravel sent up every few yards a vertical, prismatic fan, and the multicoloured drops showered over the flowers in a perfumed cloud.

MARCEL PROUST, SWANN'S WAY

This rule in gardening
never forget,
To sow dry, and set wet.

JOHN RAY, *ENGLISH PROVERBS*

Let us, then, begin by defining what a garden is, and what it ought to be. It is a piece of ground fenced off from cattle, and appropriated to the use and pleasure of man: it is, or ought to be, cultivated and enriched by art, with such products as are not natural to this country, and, consequently, it must be artificial in its treatment, and may, without impropriety, be so in its appearance; yet, there is so much of littleness in art, when compared with nature, that they cannot well be blended: it were, therefore, to be wished, that the exterior of a garden should be made to assimilate with park scenery, or the landscape of nature; the interior may then be laid out with all the variety, contrast, and even whim, that can produce pleasing objects to the eye.

HUMPHRY REPTON, *OBSERVATIONS ON THE THEORY AND PRACTICE OF LANDSCAPE GARDENING*

Brown and furry

Caterpillar in a hurry

Take your walk

To the shady leaf, or stalk

Or what not

Which may be the chosen spot.

No toad spy you,

Hovering bird of prey pass by you;

Spin and die,

To live again a butterfly.

CHRISTINA ROSSETTI, *SING-SONG*

An October Garden

In my Autumn garden I was fain
To mourn among my scattered roses;
Alas for that last rosebud which uncloses
To Autumn's languid sun and rain
When all the world is on the wane!
Which has not felt the sweet constraint of June,
Nor heard the nightingale in tune.

Broad-faced asters by my garden walk,
You are but coarse compared with roses:
More choice, more dear that
rosebud which uncloses
Faint-scented, pinched, upon its stalk,
That least and last which cold winds balk;
A rose it is though least and last of all,
A rose to me though at the fall.

CHRISTINA ROSSETTI

What is Pink?

What is pink? a rose is pink
By the fountain's brink.
What is red? a poppy's red
In its barley bed.
What is blue? the sky is blue
Where the clouds float through.
What is white? a swan is white
Sailing in the light.
What is yellow? pears are yellow,
Rich and ripe and mellow.
What is green? the grass is green,
With small flowers between.
What is violet? clouds are violet
In the summer twilight.
What is orange? why, an orange,
Just an orange!

CHRISTINA ROSSETTI

You have heard it said that flowers only flourish rightly in the garden of someone who loves them. I know you would like that to be true; you would think it a pleasant magic if you could flush your flowers into brighter bloom by a kind look upon them.

JOHN RUSKIN, *SESAME AND LILIES*

129

I know a bank whereon the wild thyme blows,
Where ox-lips and the nodding violet grows;
Quite over-canopied with luscious woodbine,
With sweet musk-roses, and with eglantine:
There sleeps Titania sometime of the night,
Lulled in these flowers with dances and delight;
And there the snake throws her enamell'd skin,
Weed wide enough to wrap a fairy in:
And with the juice of this I'll streak her eyes,
And make her full of hateful fantasies.

Take thou some of it, and seek
through this grove:
A sweet Athenian lady is in love
With a disdainful youth: anoint his eyes;
But do it when the next thing he espies
May be the lady: thou shalt know the man
By the Athenian garments he hath on.
Effect it with some care, that he may prove
More fond on her than she upon her love:
And look thou meet me ere the first cock crow.

WILLIAM SHAKESPEARE, OBERON'S SPEECH IN *A MIDSUMMER NIGHT'S DREAM*

from The Sensitive Plant

A Sensitive Plant in a garden grew,
And the young winds fed it with silver dew,
And it opened its fan-like leaves to the light.
And closed them beneath the kisses of night.

And the Spring arose on the garden fair,
And the Spirit of Love felt everywhere;
And each flower and herb on Earth's dark breast
Rose from the dreams of its wintry rest.

PERCY BYSSHE SHELLEY

You are a locked garden, my sister, my bride;
you are an enclosed spring, a sealed up fountain.
Your shoots are a royal garden full of pomegranates
with choice fruits:
henna with nard,
nard and saffron;
calamus and cinnamon with every kind of spice,
myrrh and aloes with all the finest spices.
You are a garden spring,
a well of fresh water flowing down from Lebanon.

SONG OF SOLOMON 4:12–15

from Hortulus

Though a life of retreat
offers various joys,
None, I think, will compare
with the time one employs
In the study of herbs, or
in striving to gain
Some practical knowledge
of nature's domain
Get a garden! What kind
you may get matters not.

WALAFRID STRABO

The Gardener

The gardener does not love to talk,
He makes me keep the gravel walk;
And when he puts his tools away,
He locks the door and takes the key.

Away behind the currant row,
Where no one else but cook may go,
Far in the plots, I see him dig,
Old and serious, brown and big.

He digs the flowers, green, red, and blue,
Nor wishes to be spoken to.
He digs the flowers and cuts the hay,
And never seems to want to play.

Silly gardener! summer goes,
And winter comes with pinching toes,
When in the garden bare and brown
You must lay your barrow down.

Well now, and while the summer stays,
To profit by these garden days,
O how much wiser you would be
To play at Indian wars with me!

Robert Louis Stevenson

The Blackbird

O Blackbird! Sing me something well:
While all the neighbours shoot thee round,
I keep smooth plats of fruitful ground,
Where thou may'st warble, eat and dwell.

The espaliers and the standards all
Are thine; the range of lawn and park:
The unnetted black-hearts ripen dark,
All thine, against the garden wall.

Yet, tho' I spared thee all the spring,
Thy sole delight is, sitting still,
With that gold dagger of thy bill
To fret the summer jenneting.

A golden bill! the silver tongue,
Cold February loved, is dry:
Plenty corrupts the melody
That made thee famous once, when young:

And in the sultry garden-squares,
Now thy flute-notes are changed to coarse,
I hear thee not at all, or hoarse
As when a hawker hawks his wares.

Take warning! he that will not sing
While yon sun prospers in the blue,
Shall sing for want, ere leaves are new,
Caught in the frozen palms of Spring.

Alfred, Lord Tennyson

Nearer the house was a portion given up entirely to flowers, not growing in beds or borders, but crammed together in an irregular square, where they bloomed in half-wild profusion. There were rose bushes there and lavender and rosemary and a bush apple-tree which bore little red and yellow streaked apples in later summer, and Michaelmas daisies and red-hot pokers and old-fashioned pompom dahlias in autumn and peonies and pinks already budding.

An old man in the village came one day a week to till the vegetable garden, but the flower garden was no one's especial business... the flowers grew just as they would in crowded masses, perfect in their imperfection.

FLORA THOMPSON, *LARK RISE TO CANDLEFORD*

I once had a sparrow alight upon my shoulder for a moment while I was hoeing in a village garden, and I felt that I was more distinguished by that circumstance than I should have been by any epaulet I could have worn.

HENRY DAVID THOREAU, *WALDEN;*

OR, LIFE IN THE WOODS

from Magdalen Walks

The little white clouds are racing over the sky,
And the fields are strewn with the
gold of the flower of March,
The daffodil breaks under foot, and the tasselled larch
Sways and swings as the thrush goes hurrying by.

A delicate odour is borne on the
wings of the morning breeze,
The odour of deep wet grass, and of
brown new-furrowed earth,
The birds are singing for joy of the Spring's glad birth,
Hopping from branch to branch on the rocking trees.

And all the woods are alive with the
murmur and sound of Spring,
And the rosebud breaks into pink on the climbing briar,
And the crocus-bed is a quivering moon of fire
Girdled round with the belt of an amethyst ring.

And the plane to the pine-tree is
whispering some tale of love
Till it rustles with laughter and
tosses its mantle of green,
And the gloom of the wych-elm's
hollow is lit with the iris sheen
Of the burnished rainbow throat and
the silver breast of a dove.

OSCAR WILDE

Every afternoon, as they were coming from school, the children used to go and play in the Giant's garden.

It was a large lovely garden, with soft green grass. Here and there over the grass stood beautiful flowers like stars, and there were twelve peach-trees that in the spring-time broke out into delicate blossoms of pink and pearl, and in the autumn bore rich fruit. The birds sat on the trees and sang so sweetly that the children used to stop their games in order to listen to them. 'How happy we are here!' they cried to each other.

OSCAR WILDE, *THE HAPPY PRINCE, AND OTHER TALES*

There had never been in the village such a garden as this of Evelina Adams's. All the old blooms which had come over the seas with the early colonists, and started as it were their own colony of flora in the new country, flourished there. The naturalised pinks and phlox and hollyhocks and the rest, changed a little in colour and fragrance by the conditions of a new climate and soil, were all in Evelina's garden, and no one dreamed what they meant to Evelina; and she did not dream herself, for her heart was always veiled to her own eyes, like the face of a nun. The roses and pinks, the poppies and heart's-ease, were to this maiden-woman, who had innocently and helplessly outgrown her maiden heart, in the place of all the loves of life which she had missed. Her affections had forced an outlet in roses; they exhaled sweetness in pinks, and twined and clung in honeysuckle-vines. The daffodils, when they came up in the spring, comforted her like the smiles of children; when she saw the first rose, her heart leaped as at the face of a lover.

MARY ELEANOR WILKINS FREEMAN, *EVELINA'S GARDEN*

From the oval-shaped flower-bed there rose perhaps a hundred stalks spreading into heart-shaped or tongue-shaped leaves half way up and unfurling at the tip red or blue or yellow petals marked with spots of colour raised upon the surface; and from the red, blue or yellow gloom of the throat emerged a straight bar, rough with gold dust and slightly clubbed at the end. The petals were voluminous enough to be stirred by the summer breeze, and when they moved, the red, blue and yellow lights passed one over the other, staining an inch of the brown earth beneath with a spot of the most intricate colour. The light fell either upon the smooth, grey back of a pebble, or, the shell of a snail with its brown, circular veins, or falling into a raindrop, it expanded with such intensity of red, blue and yellow the thin walls of water that one expected them to burst and disappear. Instead, the drop was left in a second silver grey once more, and the light now settled upon the flesh of a leaf, revealing the branching thread of fibre beneath the surface, and again it moved on and spread its illumination in the vast green spaces beneath the dome of the heart-shaped and tongue-shaped leaves. Then the breeze stirred rather more briskly overhead and the colour was flashed into the air above, into the eyes of the men and women who walk in Kew Gardens in July.

VIRGINIA WOOLF,
'KEW GARDENS' IN MONDAY OR TUESDAY

In the garden snowdrops, crocuses, hyacinths, magnolias, roses, lilies, asters, the dahlia in all its varieties, pear trees and apple trees and cherry trees and mulberry trees, with an enormous quantity of rare and flowering shrubs, of trees evergreen and perennial, grew so thick on each other's roots that there was no plot of earth without its bloom, and no stretch of sward without its shade.

VIRGINIA WOOLF, *ORLANDO*

151

For Orlando's taste was broad; he was no lover of garden flowers only; the wild and the weeds even had always a fascination for him.

VIRGINIA WOOLF, *ORLANDO*

from To a Butterfly

Oh! pleasant, pleasant were the days,
The time, when, in our childish plays,
My sister Emmeline and I
Together chased the butterfly!
A very hunter did I rush
Upon the prey: – with leaps and springs
I followed on from brake to bush;
But she, God love her, feared to brush
The dust from off its wings.

WILLIAM WORDSWORTH

from The Two Trees

Beloved, gaze in thine own heart,
The holy tree is growing there;
From joy the holy branches start,
And all the trembling flowers they bear.
The changing colours of its fruit
Have dowered the stars with merry light;
The surety of its hidden root
Has planted quiet in the night;
The shaking of its leafy head
Has given the waves their melody,
And made my lips and music wed,
Murmuring a wizard song for thee.

There the Loves a circle go,

The flaming circle of our days,

Gyring, spiring to and fro

In those great ignorant leafy ways;

Remembering all that shaken hair

And how the wingèd sandals dart,

Thine eyes grow full of tender care:

Beloved, gaze in thine own heart.

Gaze no more in the bitter glass

The demons, with their subtle guile,

Lift up before us when they pass,

Or only gaze a little while;

For there a fatal image grows

That the stormy night receives,

Roots half hidden under snows,

Broken boughs and blackened leaves.

For all things turn to barrenness
In the dim glass the demons hold,
The glass of outer weariness,
Made when God slept in times of old.
There, through the broken branches, go
The ravens of unresting thought;
Flying, crying, to and fro,
Cruel claw and hungry throat,
Or else they stand and sniff the wind,
And shake their ragged wings; alas!
Thy tender eyes grow all unkind:
Gaze no more in the bitter glass.

WILLIAM BUTLER YEATS

In the Seven Woods

I have heard the pigeons of the Seven Woods
Make their faint thunder, and the garden bees
Hum in the lime-tree flowers; and put away
The unavailing outcries and the old bitterness
That empty the heart. I have forgot awhile
Tara uprooted, and new commonness
Upon the throne and crying about the streets
And hanging its paper flowers from post to post,
Because it is alone of all things happy.
I am contented, for I know that Quiet
Wanders laughing and eating her wild heart
Among pigeons and bees, while that Great Archer,
Who but awaits His hour to shoot, still hangs
A cloudy quiver over Pairc-na-lee.

WILLIAM BUTLER YEATS

www.summersdale.com